f Saunton

The rocks forming the resistant promontory of Saunton Down, deposited some 400 million years ago, are being slowly broken down and washed away by the action of the sea and weather. If it is a stormy day you will appreciate the violence of the wave action attacking the cliffs. Sand eroded from the cliff will be dragged by the waves to settle in off-shore sand bars in deeper water beyond the power of the breaking waves. If the day is calmer, deposition is the dominant process as sand grains wafted shorewards by the waves are deposited on the beach, some eventually to be blown inland to form the sand dune ramparts of Braunton Burrows.

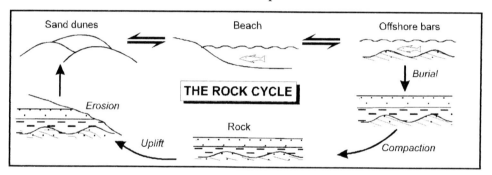

Our coastline is part of a dynamic cycle of deposition, preservation, erosion and redeposition. The off-shore sand bars and the sand dunes are destined to become the sandstones of the future. Sands become sandstones if buried and compacted under more soil or sediment. Typically hundreds of metres of sediment are required to press the grains sufficiently close together to form rock. In some cases a natural chemical 'cement' can accelerate rock formation. Eventually uplift may re-expose this sedimentary rock and the process begins all over again.

Peter Keene   Chris Cornford
Geography Unit   Hallsannery Field Centre
Oxford Brookes University   Bideford

INTRODUCTION TO INTERPRETATION

The key to the past

Looking towards the sea, most people would recognise that the composition and the shape of a beach is closely related to the waves which wash over them. Similarly, a direct relationship can be identified between the sand dunes behind the wide beach and strong on-shore winds. Both these contemporary coastal landforms can be directly related to coastal processes operating today.

However, when examining older features in the coastal landscape, such as the cliffs of Saunton Down, it is not as easy to establish how the sediments which make up these rocks were laid down, or what processes were operating at that time or what the environment looked like. Yet the clues are there, coded in the sediments we see.

One approach is to assume that the relationship between process and environment has always been the same. Recognising features (structures and textures) in ancient compacted rocks, that are also found in modern soft sediments, allows us to suggest that similar environments of deposition were present in both cases. This may seem obvious but modern geology could be said to date from 1785 when James Hutton explicitly drew attention to this relationship by proposing that "The present is the key to the past" and developed the so-called principle of 'uniformitarianism'.

This walk puts this maxim into practice. First, two modern coastal landforms (beaches and sand dunes) are linked to contemporary coastal processes. Then, by inspecting the cliff face, older scenarios are identified and a sequence of former coastal environments reconstructed to suggest a history of climatic and environmental change along this coast.

Interpreting past environments

Exposed in the cliff face are a sequence of deposits which provide evidence for some of the startling climatic oscillations which have dominated England during the last two million years (the Quaternary). Although a sequence of deposits can be readily recognised, the interpretation of the history they chronicle is a matter of some controversy amongst earth scientists. It is therefore more appropriate to offer discussion and possibilities than definitive explanations.

Taking on the role of interpreter

Instead (rather in the manner of a detective story) we have chosen to draw attention to the sometimes conflicting evidence available and then, for those who will, place the participant in the position of interpreter and speculator.

The emphasis on the outward walk is on identifying and recording the various deposits seen. On the return walk, interpretation and an appraisal of what environments these deposits may represent leads to a reconstruction of a possible sequence of events responsible for the coast we see today.

Using a log sheet

If you wish to approach the walk as an interpretive challenge, recording what you see in these cliffs, then you will find it useful to note the various deposits as they are examined. The outline of a simple record sheet, suitable for any participant, can be found on page 14. Students may prefer to use a fuller 'graphic log sheet' such as one found in Keene, 1995a (see page 45). This will need adapting as the deposits examined are not exposed conveniently as one vertical column. Thus, the conventional technique of starting from the bottom bed (oldest?) and working up, isn't always practicable here.

Start the walk by leaving the Saunton Sands car park (see rear cover map) and walk down towards the sea. If it is not an exceptionally high tide, move out a little way onto the beach.

WHAT IS THE BEACH MADE OF?

Yes, O.K. - sand; but what is sand? A strict definition is that the individual grains should have a diameter of less than 2 mm and greater than 0.0625 mm. Bigger particles are gravels, cobbles and boulders. Finer particles are silts and clays. What size are the grains at your feet? Scoop up a handful. A good way of separating sands from silts and clay is by 'feel'.

Try this:	Sands feel gritty
	Silts feel 'pasty'
	Clays feel smooth

Grains larger than sand are usually trundled to the top of the shore by waves. See how shingle and stones are trapped against the cliff foot at Saunton. Grains smaller than sand are also scarce on this beach. Whenever waves pick up fine sediments they stay suspended until they drift into calmer water, beyond the breaking waves. Breaking waves also briefly lift sand grains into suspension but most sand grains will quickly drop to the beach floor again. There it survives, even in this stormy environment. How much sand is on this beach? Have a guess. A cubic metre of sand measures 1 x 1 x 1 metre.

WHAT ARE THE GRAINS MADE OF?

You can see the coarser grains with the naked eye, but a hand lens will help. Can you see at least two different types of grain? The relatively rounded 'glassy' grains are quartz - rounded by a long life of erosion, transport and deposition in this violent environment. Most other minerals are too soft to survive long. Yet, amongst the quartz (Qz) are flaky, crushable shell fragments (calcium carbonate). Why are these not destroyed?

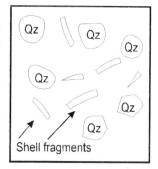

Shell fragments

SAUNTON SANDS

How much sand?

Saunton Sands stretch southwards some 5 km (5000 metres) to the combined mouth of the rivers Taw and Torridge. Conservatively we could suggest that this beach is 500 metres wide at low tide giving an area of about 2,500,000 m². In summer you could dig a two-metre pit here and still be in sand. The sand will be less deep towards the sea. Let's suggest an average depth of sand of 1 metre for the whole beach. In that case Saunton Sands has at least 2,500,000 m³ of sand in its beach store and that doesn't include the massive off-shore sand banks beyond low tide level. The sand dunes of Braunton Burrows cover another 5,000,000 m² and rise to over 30 metres in places. Even if the average depth of sand were only 5 metres that would add another 25,000,000 m³ of sand to the sum. Not a very exact figure but impressive.

Where does all this sand from?

(i) Saunton Down? In the introduction it was suggested that the erosion of Saunton Down contributes sand to the rock cycle. Is this the main source of sand? Probably not. Measurements in similar environments in Britain suggest that less than 5% of beach sediments result directly from cliff erosion. Two other contributing sources are important:

(ii) The Taw-Torridge Rivers?

Satellite pictures show river sediments belching into Bideford Bay with every outgoing tide. Most river sediments eventually find their way to the sea. Coarse sediments such as gravel and sand will be deposited near the river mouth to become part of the local sediment system including the beaches. Fine silts and muds will continue to travel off-shore to settle in calmer deep water. The rivers are an important source of sediments but the amount they contribute is not known.

(iii) Off-shore sources?

Storm waves may erode a beach, dragging sand seawards and sometimes depositing it at depths beyond the reach of normal waves so that it is no longer part of the local sediment system. On balance, waves drive sand, shells and gravel shorewards. These accumulate as sand and shell beaches or shingle banks.

However, waves can only effectively move sand shorewards in shallow water so that, if fresh stocks from off-shore are not forthcoming then, in time, the local seafloor may be swept clean and the supply of fresh beach sand declines. It is a matter of some debate as to whether, today, any significant amount of sand is arriving onto North Devon beaches from the sea bed off-shore.

Flandrian Transgression

When sea levels rose towards the end of the last ice age (the Flandrian Transgression), waves pushed accumulated frost-shattered debris and loose sediments ahead of them. By the time sea levels became relatively stable (some 3000 years ago), plentiful beaches had accumulated along substantial stretches of the world's coasts. Bideford Bay was no exception. Many earth scientists are of the opinion that this one-off 'bonus' of deposits is gradually wearing out; at a rate that is faster than natural replacement. This, they claim, is the reason for widespread examples of beach erosion around the world, otherwise a phenomena difficult to explain.

Is this shore eroding?

Those responsible for the physical management of coasts have to consider if observed changes are parts of natural cycles or may be caused by a human impact on the natural system. Is the coast at Saunton Sands eroding? How could you tell?

Moving Sand

If you felt like digging a trench into this sand you would probably find the sand is laid down in thick, flat beds parallel to the surface you are standing on. This is typical of a wide gently-sloping beach disturbed twice a day by Atlantic surf. Waves, tides and estuary currents are all agitating the sand beneath the water but are these the only processes propelling the sand?

Because the height range between high and low tide in Bideford Bay is great (8 metres), the surface of this wide, sandy beach often dries out between tides. Strong on-shore winds will disturb sand grains and bounce them up across the beach surface, a process called 'saltation'. Without shoes and socks the multiple collisions of these moving sand grains can be experienced at first hand (or rather, foot!). Some grains, determined to teach you something about wind processes, will be lifted into suspension to lodge in your hair and eyes.

The beach, then, is the source of sand for the massive dunes of Braunton Burrows. We have seen that waves exchange sand between the beach and the sea. Could there be a similar exchange between dunes and beach?

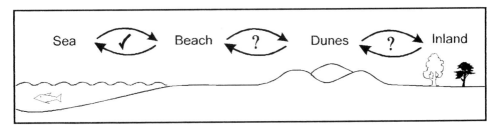

ARE THE DUNES BEING ERODED BY THE SEA?

Look towards the high tide line. The junction between sand dune and beach might provide part of the answer. Are the dunes eroding or are they gaining from the sea? What is happening in this critical zone?

EROSION? A fresh looking sand cliff is a sure sign that the sand is being undercut and removed by powerful waves at high tide.

DEPOSITION? On the other hand a bank of sand, blown up against the first sand dunes, suggests that deposition is occurring. If this deposition continued for some time then the high tide mark would gradually move seawards and the coastline would build out to sea (prograde).

BEACH PROCESSES

Saltation

Air flow over a sandy beach is slowed down by drag at the beach surface. Wind velocity is zero within a thin film of air very close to beach level. However, individual sand grains poke through this still zone into more active air. These grains can be forced forward by the wind (a) with the possibility of colliding with other grains. In this case the lighter of the two grains may then be flicked into the air (b) increasing its acceleration as it enters higher velocity wind zones. It can achieve a height of up to a metre above the ground (c) before descending in a curved trajectory to hit the ground downwind (d). Here, in the manner of a relay race, it is likely to flip other grains into the air in the same fashion (e).

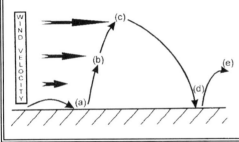

Erosion or deposition?

Looking at the junction between the beach and sand dunes you may well have been satisfied that this coast is either prograding or eroding. Which did you choose?

Old charts and maps suggest that this shoreline has been relatively stable for the past 100 years. In other words erosion has roughly balanced deposition. Perhaps that answer doesn't match your perception? This may be because your choice was determined by the time of year of your visit.

Winter 'cut'. Storm waves, occurring more frequently in winter, tend to plunge onto the beach and drag sand seawards. Such storms will cut a sharp cliff into the fore dunes at the top of the beach. Erosion is occurring.

Summer 'fill'. In calmer weather, waves gently push sand shorewards. On-shore winds will saltate dry sand up the beach to collect as a 'fill' against any 'cut' face. The 'fill' of sand forms a shallow ramp up which more sand climbs. Deposition is occurring. Storms may cut a sand cliff at any time. Has there been a storm recently?

The model below suggests that, as long as longshore movement of sand is not occurring, a form of equilibrium can develop controlled by the circulation of sand between dune and shore.

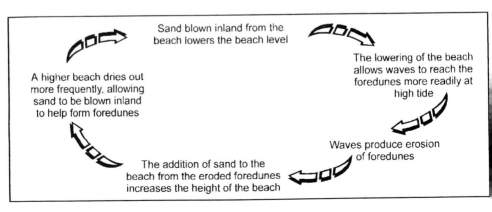

Sand blown inland from the beach lowers the beach level

The lowering of the beach allows waves to reach the foredunes more readily at high tide

A higher beach dries out more frequently, allowing sand to be blown inland to help form foredunes

Waves produce erosion of foredunes

The addition of sand to the beach from the eroded foredunes increases the height of the beach

☞ Into the Dunes

Now walk into the sand dunes through one of the gaps at the top of the beach. You might appreciate that we can not be specific about the route here, in such a dynamic changing environment. Once amongst the dunes, pause.

The soft roar of surf, so omnipresent on the beach, may now be muted. This is a place to lie and listen to sky larks. It is a very different environment from the beach yet sand still dominates the surroundings. Scoop up a handful.

DOES THIS FEEL THE SAME AS BEACH SAND?
It is probably dry rather than damp but would you expect any other differences between the sand here and that on the beach? Try looking at grain size (texture). This will involve getting your eye close to the sand. If you want to know more about 'texture' look at the table on the next page.

WHAT IS THE SAND HERE LIKE?
An examination with a hand lens would reveal that the sand here is finer than the beach sand. You could probably suggest a reason for this. Shell fragments are also more common. Mussel shells, blue-black on the outside and white on the inside, together with white razor shells are common on the beach below. You can probably pick these out.

A spectacular way of demonstrating the presence of these shell fragments is to add acid to the sand. The carbonates in the shells react immediately producing a froth of carbon dioxide bubbles. A similar experiment in the laboratory involves weighing before and after dissolving away all the carbonates. It would show that these light shell fragments form between 20 - 30% of the dune sands.

The flaky shells do not survive long in the beach surf so their common appearance on the shore and in the dunes suggests that fresh supplies from off-shore are constantly arriving on the beach. Being light, these shell fragments are easily blown inland by the wind.

What is meant by TEXTURE?

The particle size distribution and the fabric of a sediment seen on close examination.
When studying the texture of sediments at Saunton consider such questions as:

SIZE What is the dominant grain (particle) size?

SORTING To what extent has the sediment been sorted (by wind / water?) into particles of similar size (e.g. a deposit composed exclusively of fine sand is well-sorted)?

 Well sorted

 Poorly sorted

SHAPE Are the particles angular or rounded (see scale)? Water transport rounds particles but ice and movements by gravity down a slope much less so.

Rounded   Sub-rounded   Sub-angular   Angular

FABRIC What is the relationship of stones in the deposit one to another; e.g.
Do elongated stones tend to point in one direction? Preferred orientation (a).
Are stones packed together with a common dip or plunge? Imbricated (b)

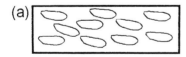

FABRIC Are stones touching each other? Clast supported (a), or
Are stones separated one from another by finer material? Matrix supported (b)

Also consider: colour, mineral type, hardness and composition.

TEXTURE: CHECKLIST CONTRASTING BEACH AND DUNE SAND

	Process	Characteristics of grains
B **E** **A** **C** **H**	**WATER** Waves washing up and down the shore	☐ Sands well-sorted by the waves but with coarse, medium and fine sands represented. ☐ Clays and silts rare on exposed shores. ☐ Grains are mostly quartz; a hard mineral able to survive constant pounding by the waves because it is resistant to fracturing. ☐ Beach sediments mature; (well-sorted, well-rounded and mainly of the same mineral (quartz). ☐ Sometimes odd rounded pebbles lie on the beach having been rolled there by waves. ☐ Shallow-water calcareous marine shell fragments well represented.
D **U** **N** **E** **S**	**WIND** Wind blowing onshore across the dry beach	☐ Very well-sorted with a small size range. ☐ Fine to medium sand dominate. Finer grains (less than 0.18 mm) have often been removed in suspension. Coarse sand is uncommon because grains larger than 0.5 mm normally fail to saltate although some coarse sand, a bed-load moved by creep, is found at base of steep avalanche slopes. ☐ Grains mainly quartz but calcareous content high (20 - 30%), composed of shell fragments blown inland from the beach. ☐ Dune sands may be more rounded than beach sands. ☐ Sand grains often pitted or frosted in appearance.

SEM IMAGE OF DUNE SANDS
A hand lens is very useful but any deeper study of sand grains requires samples to be taken back to the laboratory where they can be examined at greater magnification. This sample of Braunton Burrows dune sand has been viewed using back-scattered electron images from a scanning electron microscope (SEM). The shelly content of the sample has previously been removed using a dilute acid. By far the most common grain size (57%) was between 0.25 and 0.355 mm. (fine, medium sand). The grain surfaces are frosted and pitted.

9

☞ The Shape of the Dunes

Perhaps, nearby, there is a collapsed or slipped section of dune where the internal structure of the dune is exposed and can be examined at close hand?

The most obvious way in which dunes differ from the flat beach are the steep ridges of sand. Why are dunes the shape they are?

Uninhibited by vegetation, wind-blown sand migrates and accumulates as suggested by the sketch below, with sand saltating up the long windward slope to avalanche down the steep, sheltered (lee) side of the dune.

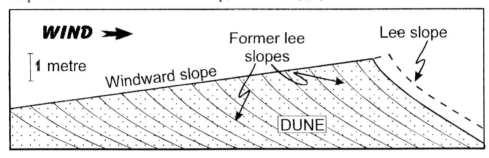

If you have found a piece of dune that has slipped away, exposing a cross section, you may be able to see part of this layered internal structure (dune bedding). Faint lines within the dune indicate rapid addition of sand followed by long periods of non-deposition. From the direction of layering you should be able to work out the direction of transport and hence the dominant wind direction.

In hot dry deserts, dunes in silhouette look much like the sketch above. However, in damper temperate coastal areas like Braunton Burrows, vegetation such as marram grass, substantially modifies dune shapes so that most dunes in this area are steeper on their seaward face.

Large scale dune-bedding with steep (30°) avalanche slopes is the characteristic internal structure of sand dunes. It can survive long after the dunes become inactive or become buried and lose their distinctive shape. It is therefore a useful indicator with which to identify ancient sand dunes.

What is meant by   STRUCTURE?

Here we are concerned mainly with the presence (or lack of) sedimentary structures such as beds. Characteristics such as cross stratification, trace fossils and ripple marks can indicate the environment of deposition. Faults and folds might reveal something of the subsequent history of the deposit. When studying the structure of sediments at Saunton consider such questions as:

BEDS   Can you detect any sheet-like structures (layering, bedding) in the deposit under examination? A bed is a distinct sheet of sediment having common textural characteristics. Beds are separated from one another by surfaces (bedding planes) which mark breaks in sedimentation.

CROSS STRATIFICATION

Are there beds (stratification) dipping at an angle to the main bedding direction? This cross stratification can be caused by the movement of ripples or on a large scale by the movement of dunes where sand avalanches down the lee slope. Cross stratification can also be caused by the infilling of hollows, similar to avalanching foreset beds in a delta. Cross stratification can indicate ancient current directions (palaeocurrents).

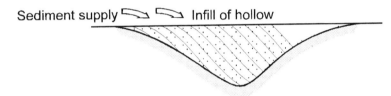

Sediment supply   Infill of hollow

RIPPLES   Are the ripple marks symmetrical (formed under wave activity) or asymmetric (formed by wind or water moving in one direction)? Ripple marks commonly occur on bedding surfaces. If deposition is occurring, the down-stream or down-wind migration of ripples can form cross stratification.

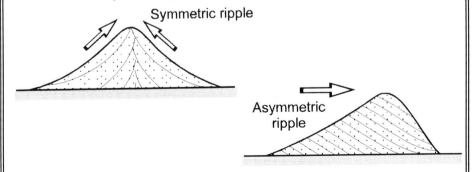

Symmetric ripple

Asymmetric ripple

Also consider post-depositional deformation such as faults, joints, folding and slumping.

STRUCTURE CHECKLIST CONTRASTING BEACH AND DUNE SAND

	Main process involved	Characteristic Structures
B E A C H	Waves washing up and down the sea shore (water)	☐ The constant swash and backwash of the waves produces thick (massive) near-horizontal beds. ☐ Low sand ridges (bars) may cause other structures such as low angle cross-strata, in truncated sets, as hollows are infilled with sand by waves, currents or tides. ☐ Ripple marks are often asymmetric, the steeper (downstream) side indicating the direction of water flow. However, wave ripples preserved on beaches may be symmetrical, reflecting the constant current reversal as waves pass overhead.
D U N E S	Wind blowing onshore across the beach (wind)	☐ Large wind-blown dunes grow and move by sand avalanching down the lee slope creating massive dune-bedding. ☐ The characteristic thick cross-strata sets have high dip angles. The angle of rest of land sand-dune avalanches (30° common) will be significantly steeper than cross-strata formed under water (usually less than 25°). ☐ Unlike desert dunes, in damp temperate climates the shape of dunes is much modified by vegetation (e.g. marram grass) so that on Braunton Burrows most dunes have a steeper seaward slope.

If you become interested in the ecology of the sand dunes and its relationship to landforms, then you should walk the "Braunton Burrows Ecology Trail" (see further reading, Page 45).

Now make your way back to the beach and turn north (right). Walk to the northern end of the beach. Below the cliff-top houses, the cliff falls directly to the beach. Facing the cliff, move left (west) until the sand, cliff and solid rock meet at a small 'nose' or promontory in the cliff face.

So far, we have looked at two modern coastal environments. The cliffs are the first piece of 'solid' rock, important in helping to build up our picture of the past. In fact, the cliffs here are not very 'solid' at all, so either stand back or wear a helmet if approaching any areas of doubtful safety. There have been many cliff failures here in the past. Landslides often bury the 'true' cliff face under loose debris which subsequently becomes vegetated.

Look at the sediments in the cliff face. Notice that they are not the same all the way up. The lower cliff is a pale, yellowish colour whilst the rather darker upper cliff looks more like a stony soil. Major differences like this mean that for interpretation we must divide the cliff face up into 'units', treating each part separately. For convenience we will call these units:

UPPER CLIFF   (UC)

LOWER CLIFF   (LC)

If you wish to note what you see and interpret the results, then the record sheet overleaf might be useful. The sheet has labelled panels for all the sediments you are likely to see on this walk. The oldest sediment is likely to be at the bottom of the column, but it is not the first sediment we examine. Notice also that the record sheet divides 'description' into TEXTURE and STRUCTURE so try to view exposures on two scales:

1   From just a few centimetres (to see textures). Hand lens?
2   From a distance of several metres or more (to see structures).

Begin by examining the 'yellow' unit (labelled LC on the record sheet). Questions which you might consider include: What is this part of the cliff made of? Pick a bit off or rub your finger over the surface. Try the sand / silt / clay test. What structures can be identified? Are these sediments recent? In what sort of environment were these sediments deposited?

RECORD OF CLIFF BEDS or UNITS   SAUNTON CLIFFS

unit	DESCRIPTION (notes)		INTERPRETATION	
	texture	structure	environment of deposition	age
UC				
MC				
LC				
E ‡				
SP			Rocky shore platform cut into Pilton Shales which continues under all overlying beds in the cliff so must be older than these. Ancient raised shore platform.	

‡ seen later in walk.

The Lower Cliff (LC)

What texture and structures did you discover in the lower cliff? A close examination suggests that much of the cliff in front to you is made of sand. Clearly this cliff sand is not being deposited today - it is hard (sometimes called sand-rock), the grains being cemented together in some way.

Determining how this sand was laid down would be one step in reconstructing the history of this coast.

What do you think was the main process involved? At this site thick parallel beds of sand dominate. However, here, or later in the walk, you may also find some of the structures illustrated overleaf. These all provide good clues to the origins of this sediment.

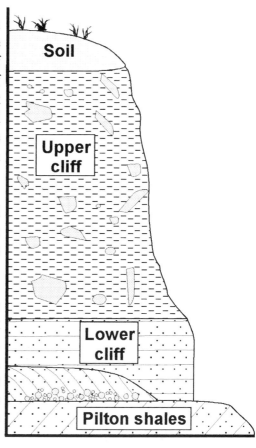

Soil

Upper cliff

Lower cliff

Pilton shales

Caption for upper photograph overleaf ▶
In places the sand-rock shows cross stratification, a characteristic of grains sorted by flow. Both wind and water flow create cross-strata. In this case the coarseness of the sand and the presence of some beds of even coarser sediments suggest deposition from water, here flowing from right to left (see page 11). Isolated pebbles and fossil shell fragments in these sands all suggest a sea shore deposit.

Caption for lower photograph overleaf ▶
These beds of coarse gravel and small pebbles may be a 'LAG', a deposit left after the finer sediments have been removed by wind or water. The way some of these deposits are packed (imbricated, see page 8) suggests that they may have formed in a stream, perhaps one meandering across a beach - Can you see a modern equivalent?

For comments on structure and texture see previous page

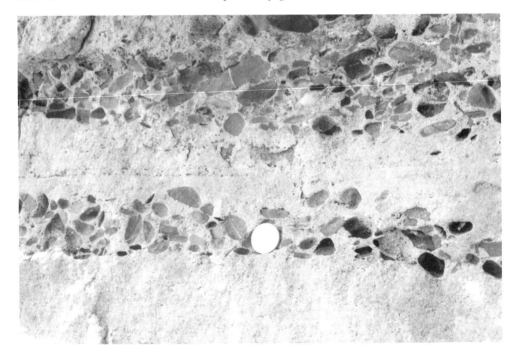

The Middle Cliff (MC)

The sand-rock of the lower cliff is usually interpreted as an ancient beach, although you might ask why a beach is found in a position that is well above the reach of waves. The sand-rock can be followed along the cliff-foot throughout the walk and beyond. Occasionally, this zone of sand-rock thickens and, above the supposed beach deposits, some rather different sand structures are visible. Let us call these the Middle Cliff (MC).

The best Middle Cliff structures are developed a little to the west, beyond the scope of this walk. The photograph below shows some Middle Cliff structures near Down End. Here the beds tilt dramatically. A 1.3 metre tripod provides a scale and also a horizontal marker against which the angle of dip of these beds can be estimated. Given these two characteristics what environment of deposition would you suggest for these beds?

The impressive scale and steep angle of dip of these beds (30°), might suggest the avalanche slope of a large sand-dune. The structure might suggest this but what about the size of sand grains? Overleaf is a sand sample taken from the Middle Cliff.

The World in a Grain of Sand

The scanning electron microscope (SEM) gives us a glimpse into a different world. The circle in the photograph below is the size of a head of a pin (diameter 1 mm). At this magnification, the size and shape of individual grains can be studied as well as tell-tale pitting caused by wear.

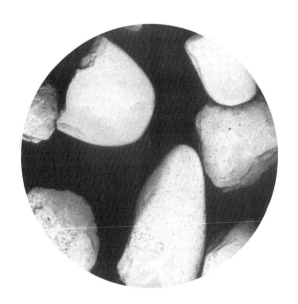

This sand sample was taken from the Middle Cliff and is similar to Braunton Burrows dune sand (shown at a different scale on page 9) and supports the idea that the Middle Cliff sands are fossil sand dunes. You may choose to note this on your record sheet on page 14.

COMPARING SAND GRAIN SIZES AT FOUR LOCAL SITES

Middle Cliff structures illustrated on page 17, might suggest a sand-dune origin for these beds. You may not have the opportunity to test this suggestion against textural evidence. However, (luckily!), we already have samples of sand collected from the Middle Cliff.

As part of a recent field exercise, students were asked to compare the texture and structure of sand from four local sites: (1) Braunton Burrows, (2) Saunton beach, (3) Saunton cliffs (lower unit), (4) Saunton cliffs (middle unit). The graph below summarises grain size results from samples collected at the four sites.

Using the graph, can you describe the grain size and degree of sorting of the sand sample taken from the Middle Cliff?

How does Middle Cliff sand compare with sand from the other three samples? Which does it most closely match?

There is a full student discussion of this graph overleaf but try considering what these results might tell you before turning over.

Note: These samples represent analysis after the calcareous (shell) content has been removed.

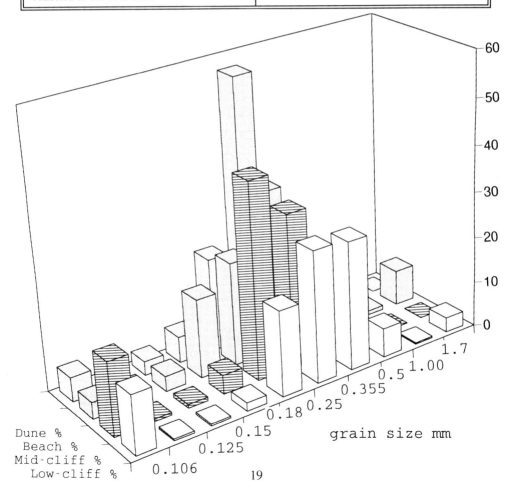

Like many field experiments, the results of analysing the sand size distribution was not as clear cut as the students would have liked! However, their discussion and conclusions are listed below. Are these similar to yours?

Beach and Lower Cliff

☐ Sand grains coarser than that moved by normal winds (over 0.5 mm) are found in both the modern beach and lower cliff sample (10%). Beds of small pebbles (not sampled) are also present in the lower cliff.

☐ Although all samples could be described as well-sorted the sorting of beach and lower cliff samples is similar and neither are as well-sorted as the modern dunes or middle cliff.

☐ The similarities between the samples from the lower cliff and the modern beach suggests that the lower cliff is a fossil beach (a palaeomarine environment) but the strongest evidence for this comes from beach structures found in the lower cliff including symmetrical ripples and small-scale, cross-stratification together with typical shallow-water, marine shells.

☐ The high proportion of fine material in the lower cliff sample (10% was finer than 0.106 mm) does not fit a beach origin well. It could be that these fines (small particles) have percolated down from the upper cliff which contains a high proportion of fines. They may therefore be regarded as a contaminant.

Dune and Middle Cliff

☐ 99 % of the sand grains in both these samples was finer than 0.5 mm, the cut-off point for normal wind transport, except for 'creep', along the ground.

☐ Coarse sand (creep, bedload) is missing from this dune-crest sample.

☐ Both these samples were very well-sorted. 57% of the dune sand was between 0.25 - 0.355 mm (medium sand moved by saltation). Finer sand is not well represented. Has it been lifted into suspension and blown further inland? This could be tested in the dunes.

☐ The Middle Cliff sands correlate more closely with the modern dune sands than any other sample. However, the suggestion that the Middle Cliff is a fossil sand dune is most strongly supported by the massive, steeply-dipping (30°) bedding found in several places in the Middle Cliff.

☐ A high proportion of marine shells was found in all four samples.

☐ The middle cliff, like the lower cliff, has an anomalously high, very fine content (16%). The reason for this could be the same in both cases.

Student survey team: Sarah Hewitt, Adela Fazel, Nathalie Johns and Charlotte O'Sullivan (Oxford Brookes University, Undergraduate Coastal Geomorphology Project, 1994)

Check for an incoming tide before even thinking of walking along the cliff-foot.

The sand-rock cliff is capped by the thick stony upper cliff (UC) noted earlier. We will consider this unit a little later. All units outcrop along the cliff-face to the west.

Now walk west for some 50 metres and out onto the rocky shore.

What is this rock like? You could use the same techniques as before:
Close up   (texture)   - grain size - hardness - colour?
Stand back   (structure)   - beds - ripples - faults - folding?

This is a fine-grained rock made originally from soft silts and clays but now a compact hard, resistant rock called the Pilton Shales. Did you identify any bedding structure? Unlike those in the cliff, these beds tilt at crazy angles, slanting steeply into, or rising sharply from the ground. This is evidence of a tortuous past of compression, folding and faulting within the earth's crust.

If you are lucky you may find marine fossil sea lilies (crinoids). Fossils such as these tell us that the Pilton Shales are ancient, probably some 365 million years old (the Devonian Period).

Folded beds are well exposed here because waves have cut a gently sloping step (a shore platform) into the Pilton Shales. As you clamber over rock and gullies, you may not appreciate the almost-horizontal nature of this marine knife-slice. This is because, subsequently, the less resistant beds of rock have been worn away more quickly than harder beds. It is also a question of scale. The near-horizontal nature of the shore platform is clear if you look at the air photo of this coast, overleaf (Saunton Down; Down End). Notice how ancient fault lines running along the rocky shore create lines of weakness which, when exploited by wave action, become long, straight gullies. Can you see examples of this near where you stand?

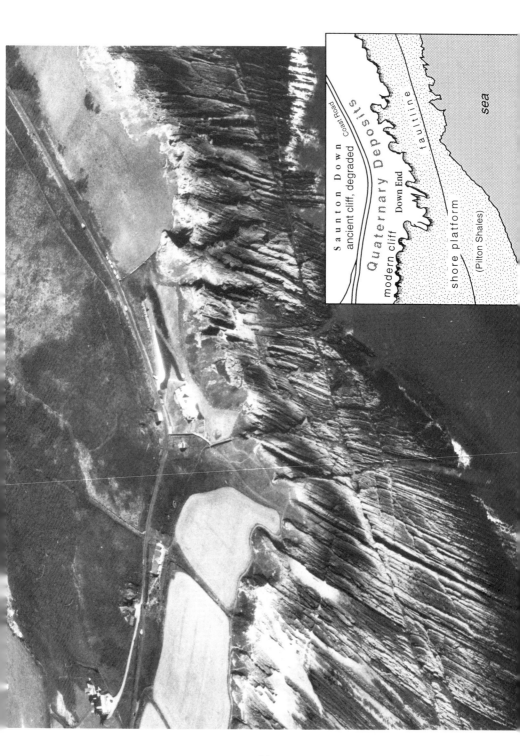

Saunton Down

ancient cliff, degraded   Coast Road

Quaternary Deposits

modern cliff   Down End

faultline

shore platform

(Pilton Shales)

sea

Now move back towards the cliff. With a little agility, and perhaps some deviations, see if you can reach the cliff foot without leaving the Pilton shales? It is possible.

What happens to the Pilton Shales when you reach the cliff face?

So - the rocky shore platform disappears into the cliff, beneath the sand-rock (LC & MC). What is the significance of this? The sand-rock must be younger than the shore platform cut by the sea. You may find convincing proof of this if nearby you find fossil acorn barnacles (as above), still in their growth position but sealed in by sand-rock, which was clearly laid down on top of them. This sort of acorn barnacle is usually found below the low water mark. What are they doing up here?

Survey boreholes show that the ancient shore platform of Pilton Shales continues some way under the sand-rock, but then rises steeply to the surface, to re-emerge along the line of the coast road (see air photo opposite). The Pilton Shale is evident in several cuttings and small quarries along the coast road. The relationship between the ancient Pilton Shales and the more recent sand-rock is also illustrated overleaf.

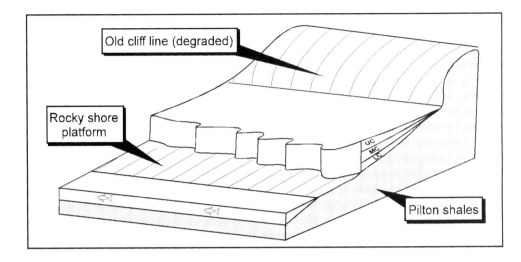

Old cliff line (degraded)

Rocky shore platform

UC
MC
LC

Pilton shales

The rocky shore platform you are standing on was eroded by marine processes, yet much of it may be a fossil landform, carved by waves at a time when sea-level was higher than today. What evidence can you see for this? Some of this evidence may be at your feet.

LOCAL EVIDENCE for HIGHER SEA-LEVELS

1 Raised shore platforms

Notice how in places the shore platform takes a step up (like a mini-cliff) onto a slightly higher platform. If the height of a platform correlates with several others alongshore, then each step could be related to a former higher sea-level. Here, on the Saunton shore, a platform has been cut at about one metre above present day normal high tide level (5 metres O.D.*). Further west remnants of platforms at 7.5 m O.D. and 13.7 m O.D. have been recognised. These platforms slope towards the sea and some alongshore, so these figures are not meant to be accurate indicators of the precise height of former sea-levels.

*   O.D. = Ordnance Datum. This is mean sea level, as used on Ordnance Survey maps. It is midway between the high and low water mark.

2 Lichens growing on the platform

The greeny-yellow terrestrial lichens on the upper shore platform shows that this area is above the level where salt water waves today cover or erode the shore at normal high tide.

3 Low tide acorn barnacles

The present high tide location of these low-water fossil acorn barnacles suggests they lived at a time when sea-level was several metres higher than today.

4 Old cliff line

The sloping shore platform disappears inland, beneath the sand-rock. As you can see from the block diagram above, it terminates abruptly against what must be a fossil sea cliff, the base of which is approximately 4 metres above today's normal high tide mark. This could have been cut at a time when sea-level was some 8 metres higher than the present day (+ 8 metres O.D.).

The Ups and Downs of the Sea

We are familiar with the daily rhythm of tides which wash our shores every 12 hours but, because of the vast time scale involved, may not be familiar with another great regular oscillation of the sea; that caused by ice ages.

During the last two million years or so (the Quaternary), ice ages have come and gone roughly every 100,000 years. The ice caps were fed by extracting (and for the time being not returning) water from the oceans. Such interruptions of the water cycle can cause world sea-levels to fall between 100 - 120 metres.

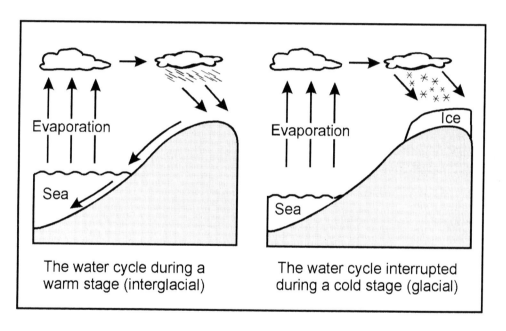

The water cycle during a warm stage (interglacial)

The water cycle interrupted during a cold stage (glacial)

At the peak of the last ice age (about 18,000 years ago) a palaeolithic hunter standing on the crest of Saunton Down would not have seen the sea. It would have retreated to beyond the horizon. During warm stages (interglacials) when the water cycle is partly restored, the sea comes flooding back. The text box overleaf explains why sea-levels during past warm (interglacial) stages may have been even higher than today.

Upset water cycle

World sea-levels may only remain stable as long as the water cycle is uninterrupted (see above). During cold stages of the Quaternary (the last two million years), 5% of the world's land surface was so cold that a proportion of each winter's snowfall failed to melt in spring and instead packed down to form glacier ice, thickening year by year. This upset the water cycle, insufficient water returning to the sea to balance losses due to evaporation. The many cold stages in the Quaternary have therefore been times of low world sea-level.

Yo-yo oscillations

The periodic growth and decline of ice caps during the Quaternary caused repeated fluctuations in world sea-level of between 100 and 120 metres. Such yo-yo oscillations, on balance occurring about every 100,000 years, meant that shores were repeatedly abandoned by the sea during glaciations (G) only to be revisited at the height of the next interglacial (I). Today we are experiencing one such interglacial revisitation.

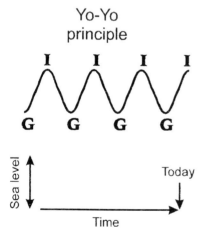

Descending staircase

World sea-levels are not only affected by the growth and decay of ice caps (glacio-eustatic changes), but are linked to a host of other complex changes. For example, plate tectonic movements are, at present, slowly increasing the capacity of ocean basins, superimposing on the yo-yo fluctuations a steady slow fall in world sea-level. This could produce a straircase effect, the height of each interglacial sea-level not quite matching the preceding one.

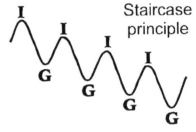

Some earth scientists calculate that this should mean that sea-levels today are some 8 metres lower than during the last interglacial (the Ipswichian). Remnants of fossil beaches surviving from that time (125,000 years ago) can, therefore, sometimes be located, perched a few metres above present mean sea-level.

The future

Since ice sheets have survived in Antarctica for the whole of the Quaternary it is doubtful if the water cycle could ever be regarded as 'in balance'. Melting ice continues to cause sea-level to rise, augmented now by the expansion of sea water, indirectly warmed by carbon dioxide releases from an increasingly industrialised society (the greenhouse effect). Local coastal planners need to consider an appropriate response to sea-levels rising at perhaps 4 mm a year, the thickness of one domestic building brick (2½") every 16 years.

☞ The Upper Cliff (UC)

Now move to a place nearby which gives you a reasonable view of the Upper Cliff (UC), above the sand-rock. This was described earlier as looking like a stony soil. Choose a section that is free from vegetation and land slips.

It is an inaccessible part of the cliff but the photograph below may help you to recognise some characteristics of the Upper Cliff from where you stand. Before turning overleaf, if you want to continue in your role of interpreter, ask yourself the following questions. What shape are the stones in the Upper Cliff (page 8)? Are the stones really distributed randomly or do they have some pattern (fabric) that you can recognise? Are the particles well-sorted or not? Can you recognise any structure (page 11)?

When you have noted as much as you can, consult the detailed description overleaf. This was achieved by a closer and longer examination than you can attempt now. If you wished you could undertake a closer inspection when you pass stop 3 on your return journey.

Description of the Upper Cliff

Some points noted from a close examination of the upper cliff. How many of these were you able to recognise?

☐ STRUCTURE   No signs of beds or stratification (page 11).

☐ SIZE   Particle sizes range all the way from stones to clay.

☐ SORTING   An unsorted jumble of all sizes.

☐ SHAPE   All the stones are very angular (page 8).

☐ STONE TYPE   (lithology)   Most of the stones are relatively soft shale. All the stones appear to be of local origin (i.e. similar to Pilton Shales which includes some sandstones and limestones).

☐ FABRIC   Most of the stones tend NOT to be touching one another or packed together. Rather, they are 'floating' within a matrix of finer material. They are 'matrix supported' (page 8).

☐ FABRIC   Many of the longer stones seem to be pointing out of the cliff. They have a preferred orientation (page 8). The preferred orientation here is very marked and is at right angles to the crest of Saunton Down (i.e. down slope). This characteristic can be recognised by eye but a detailed survey could confirm this. The text box opposite explains how such surveys are carried out.

The description above should make it possible to interpret what you can see to suggest what processes were responsible for depositing the material found in the Upper Cliff and to consider what climatic conditions prevailed at that time. Any ideas of your own before reading on?

Stones with a preferred orientation?

If the longer stones in an unconsolidated cliff exposure are examined closely, many may appear to be pointing in a common direction. Examining the 'preferred orientation' of the long axis of a sample of stones can be useful, both to suggest the environment of deposition of the material and a possible direction of flow after initial formation.

Equipment needed

1) Plastic (not steel) knitting needle
2) Spade and trowel (to clean site)
3) Prismatic or orienteering compass
4) Ruler or tape (5) Helmet (6) Inclinometer

Selecting the sampling site

To avoid more recent surface distortions choose a vertical face at least a metre below the surface soil. The face must look stable enough to work without fear of cliff falls. Helmets must be worn. Expose a clean face by removing collapsed or loose debris. Select a square metre of face, where the material appears to have common characteristics. Identify stones which are at least 3 cm long and look as if they have a measurable long axis (i.e. length exceeds width). A sample of 30 to 50 stones should give good results.

Measuring stone orientation

(i)   If, as here, the site cannot be disturbed (as it an SSSI), then simply lay a knitting needle in sympathy with the perceived long axis of the stone, replicating the orientation and dip of the stone without disturbing it. This method gives quite acceptable results.

(ii)   A more accurate method, for use when suitable, is to carefully remove appropriate stones from the cliff face one by one, leaving an undisturbed cast in the face. Within the preserved cast (impression), replicate the orientation and dip of the long axis of the stone with a plastic knitting needle.

A compass can now be used to measure the compass orientation (0-360°) of the knitting needle (pointing down dip). If required, the angle of dip (inclination) of the needle can also be measured using an inclinometer. Repeat this task between 30 and 50 times!

Tabling the results

Results may be tabled as follows:
(a) Compass orientation of long axis (0-360°).
(b)   Angle of dip. Angle that long axis of stones makes with the horizontal (0-90°).
(x)   Class. Group the compass directions (0-360°) into classes of 30° (see below).

360° listed as 30° classes; the mid-point of each class is shown in brackets, see (x).
000-029 (015), 030-059 (045), 060-089 (075), 090-119 (105), 120-149 (135), 150-179 (165),
180-209 (195), 210-239 (225), 240-269 (255), 270-299 (285), 300-329 (315), 330-359 (345).

Example of the beginning of a table listing results

	(a) compass orientation (0-360°) of long axis of stones, pointing down dip	(x) Add after field visit. Group results (a) into classes of say 30° e.g: 000-029 (015)	(b) angle of dip of long axis (0 - 90°)
1	022	015	17
2	094	105	10

A Rose Diagram

To help interpretation, results can be presented visually, in the form of a rose diagram (polar coordinate graph paper can make constructing this very easy).

A rose diagram can take various forms. The one illustrated below plots the orientation of the stones measured as a compass direction (in the direction towards which the stones dip). Direction lines were drawn from the centre of the rose to lengths proportional to the number of stones falling into any 30° directional class. The number of stones in each class then determines the extent of shading of the rose.

Saunton 'Upper Cliff' site

The rose below was drawn from data plotted and interpreted by Martin Melges, Karen Parker, Guy Pluckwell and Mike Woods, (Coastal Geomorphology student project 1994). For further detail on preferred orientation exercises see Keene (1995a).

Interpretation

The rose diagram confirms what may have been suspected by observation, that a strong preferred orientation exists. This together with lithological evidence (all stones are local) and evidence from the fabric (it is a matrix supported sediment) all support the idea that this is a classic 'head' deposit, a slope deposit which is commonly the product of processes active in a cold periglacial, tundra-like environment. Such conditions existed in southern Britain at the peak of the last ice age, 18,000 years ago.

Significance of dip

Stones exhibiting a preferred orientation may also dip in a common direction. They often dip downwards in the direction from which the 'flow' has come (i.e. up-stream, up-glacier or up-slope). The stones here 'dip' inland implying that the material moved down the slope from Saunton Down.

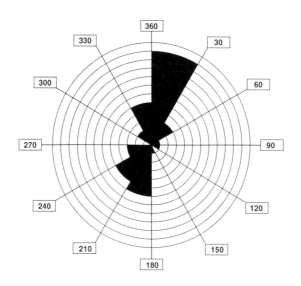

TRANSPORT PROCESSES IN THE UPPER CLIFF

Is this simply a rotten old cliff?

Rocks weathered at the earth's surface often decay into a mantle of waste without involving movement. However, if this cliff had simply 'rotted' in situ we would expect to see traces of the original rock structure. The absence of structure and the unsorted jumble of rock fragments of several different types, 'floating' in a finer matrix, all suggest a transported deposit.

What transport process was involved?

X   **WATER?** Some key indicators of water transport are missing:
Stones are all angular, not rounded.
There is no sorting by size into beds.
There is no selection by rock type. Soft shales seem to have survived as well as harder rocks. An immature deposit.

X   **ICE?** Glacial till deposited beneath ice sheets has similar matrix-supported, unsorted, lithologically immature characteristics but the dominance of very local material (no erratics), and the absence or other signs of glacial activity makes it an unlikely choice.

X   **LANDSLIDE?** Catastrophic slope failures produce unsorted, angular debris composed of local (up-slope) material. However, instant rock falls do not favour such well-developed down-slope preferred orientation of stones as here.

✓ **SOLIFLUCTION** More gradual hillside movement such as the down-slope flow of saturated sub-soil (solifluction) fit all the characteristics listed, including the stone orientation. Such slope deposits, locally called 'head', are very common on foot slopes throughout the district.

What conditions favour solifluction?

Although movement of material on slopes is occurring today, the extensive mantles of 'head' found on slopes throughout the district suggest that slope movements were once much more active. Mass movement on this scale is associated with cold climates, where conditions for solifluction are optimal. Most authorities link local solifluction deposits to the coldest part of the last ice age, some 18,000 years ago. Then, North Devon was a tundra-like wilderness with a mean annual air temperature about 10^0C colder than today. At that time, mass movement of soil and hillside rock debris, even down quite gentle slopes, was much faster (in the order of 10-100 mm a year). Slope movements today (soil creep) averages 1-2 mm a year.

Why was slope transport so much more effective in those days?

☐   In the 'arctic' climate the ground was permanently frozen (permafrost), only the top metre or so briefly melting out each summer (the active layer). Permafrost provided a barrier to the downward infiltration of water into the ground so that in summer the active layer became extremely moist, unstable slurry with high pore pressures.

☐   Permafrost acted as a lubricating surface over which the active layer could easily flow, sludging downslope in an unsorted mess of debris of all sizes. Within this water-saturated mess, any elongated stones would gradually become aligned within the flow so that their compass orientation would be parallel to the direction of movement of the debris within which they were embedded.

☐   Freeze-thaw activity detached fresh rock each winter and frost-heave caused the downhill movement of this debris under the influence of gravity.

☞ Towards the Cave

The three main units of the cliff have now been introduced (and recorded on page 14?). Now make your way westwards, towards the entrance of the shallow cave illustrated.

Notice as you walk, that you have to cross one or more gullies with green algae (seaweed) *Enteromorpha* spp. growing in it. Take care - this is slippery! Look more closely in the water and you may find some fish.

Standing in the gully and looking along the trough towards the sea, you may wonder what could form this linear 'trench', cutting down into the hard Pilton beds? As we have previously noted (page 21), these gullies in the shore platform often follow the lines of faults (fractures), where the broken rock is more easily eroded. The green algae thrive in water that is brackish rather than salt. This suggests that a fresh-water spring from the cliff flows this way. Is there any other evidence of this?

FRESH WATER FROM THE CLIFF

You may have noted that the sand-rock in this cliff area, near the gully, is far from stable. Not only is it breaking away but the whole area forms a bay. This appears to be true wherever we see green algae in gullies! Is there a link?

Hard Water

The water here is not only fresh, rather than salty, but it is also 'hard'. Hard water contains dissolved limestone or calcium carbonate. Evidence of this may be found around the edges of the pools in this area where you may find a white crust of 'tufa', lime that has come out of the water upon evaporation. Where did this lime come from? The fresh water, filtering through the sand-rock and gathering in the fault gully, has picked up (dissolved) the carbonate from the shell fragments.

Cliff failure

The sand-rock in the cliff in this area is no longer nearly horizontal but has sagged into a roughly concave structure. How can solid rock have 'collapsed' like this? When we remember that the sand-rock normally contains 20% - 30% shell carbonate, and that the carbonate forms the 'cement' holding the ancient sand-rock together, we have a ready explanation of both the 'sagging' of the beds and the crumbly, uncemented nature of the cliff.

☞ Into the Cave stop 7

Now complete your walk across the rocks to the cave seen on the other side of the shallow bay.

Here is another chance to look at some fascinating sand-rock structures. Try working out which direction the current was flowing. Why is this cave here? What controls its shape? Rub your finger against the cliff face. Is the sand-rock sand or rock? Or both and if so why?

IS SAND-ROCK SAND OR ROCK?

Some of the sand is so soft that it looks like yesterday's beach. Yet some sand, seemingly of the same origin, is hard and rock-like (sand-rock). As described earlier, water percolating through the shell-rich beds of overlying sands, has provided calcium carbonate which, in places, has cemented the sand into a resistant sand-rock. In other places sand-rock previously cemented has been de-calcified again. Caves and other irregularities in the cliff face can be related to differential erosion controlled by the relative resistance of the cemented beds.

Sand Pipes

Nearby, you may have seen some peculiar pipe-shaped features in the sand-rock. The photograph shows a well preserved example but others have been partly eroded by the sea. Lateral thinking may be needed to come up with some good idea about the origin of these features. Think about this before reading on.

SAND PIPES

DESCRIPTION
Occasionally, in various stages of erosion, you may identify along the sand cliff, cylindrical tubes up to a metre in diameter, similar to the one in the photo. The ribbed sides of these pipes are invariably of hard sand-rock. Yet, where not eroded, the pipe is filled with soft non-calcareous sand. The pipes do not extend into the 'head' above and terminate close to the beach where sometimes 'spills' of cemented sand may be seen issuing from the base. The origin of these pipes is not certain and your ideas may be better than ours. If you have a better idea consider how you would test it!

OUR INTERPRETATION
The loose non-calcareous sand within the pipe suggests that this sand has been decalcified at some time.

Initially, the site of a pipe might simply have been a preferential channel for ground water percolating downwards. This water, particularly if it was rather acidic, would gradually dissolve out the calcareous cement of the sand-rock, leaving only a soft unconsolidated sand. This would remain until, exposed by cliff erosion, the loose sand was free to escape. The hard 'spills' seen at the base of some pipes might represent redeposition of the calcareous cement as saturated water left the base of the pipe.

Continue to make your way west for some 200 metres until you come across a huge pink boulder embedded in the cliff foot. Use the front cover photo to locate this giant boulder. Note the climber for scale! He is 2 cm tall. The rock is 2½ metres long.

Does this boulder look like part of the local Pilton Shales? If your answer is "yes", its probably time you had a rest!

However, questions which might come to mind include.
1 What is this boulder made of?
2 Is it older/ younger / same age as (a) Pilton Shales (b) the sand-rock.
3 Is it in situ or has it been transported in some way?
4 If it has been transported then by what and from where?

Have a good look at this remarkable giant before reading on.
Some questions can be answered promptly - others are more difficult.

A TRANSPORTED FOREIGN BODY
This is a pink / red foliated GRANITE. As granite is an igneous rock which forms in a molten state deep underground, there is no way that this isolated, rather rounded boulder can be in situ. It must therefore have come from somewhere else.

RELATIVE AGE
The boulder is sitting on the shore platform of Pilton Shales. It must therefore have been 'placed' here after the shore platform was cut. These platforms are assumed to have been carved by high sea-levels during a warm interval (an interglacial) within the Quaternary. The boulder is partly covered by the raised beach deposit (sand-rock) which covers part of this shore platform. It therefore arrived sometime after the shore platform was cut but before the sand-rock was laid down - but how?

BOULDER TRANSPORT   Options?

What are the options? This could be called a multiple-hypothesis testing situation or it could be called a game! Either way, before reading on, consider which is the most probable mode of transport for this boulder. Try giving a probability score out of ten for the following potential candidates:

- ☐ meteorite
- ☐ human
- ☐ slope processes
- ☐ aeolian (wind)
- ☐ marine (sea)
- ☐ rivers
- ☐ ice cap (glaciers)
- ☐ icebergs

METEORITE Nice idea - wrong sort of rock. Probability score: zero!

SLOPE PROCESSES such as solifluction are quite capable of carrying large boulders down-slope, but only from a local, up-slope location. To get this non-local rock into the district in the first place would require an earlier transporting agent. Score?

WIND Rather low on our probability scale!

HUMAN Sailing ships in ballast often carried exotic stones from far shores and dumped these upon reaching home estuaries. Alternatively didn't large stones make their way from Wales to Stonehenge? However the problem is age. As this boulder is sealed in beneath 'head' and sand-rock. What is the most recent time it could have arrived?

RIVERS This boulder weighs about 13 tonnes. In the 1952 Lynmouth floods, 50 tonne boulders were on the move. There is no doubt streams are capable of transporting boulders of this size but again there is the problem of source. The characteristics of this boulder do not match those of the nearest granites, those of Lundy or Dartmoor. Perhaps the highest score so far but probably not worth betting on.

MARINE PROCESSES Currents and tides are non-starters. Wave energy is effective at the surface but cannot move coarse material at depth. This water-rounded boulder was probably rolled by waves as it sat on the rocky shore platform. Boulders move alongshore until trapped in a bay but long distance wave transport is unlikely.

ICE CAPS (GLACIERS) Glaciers can move rocks hundreds of miles, dropping them well outside the rock's original home. Such 'erratics' can be used to plot areas of former glaciation long after the ice sheet has melted. If there is evidence which supports a former glaciation of this area then the idea of ice transport looks good.

ICEBERGS Did you imagine a boulder sliding off a giant iceberg which had grounded at Saunton? What sort of score did it get? Well, no problems with the mechanism; the Atlantic floor off Greenland has trails of 'drop stones' (some the size of houses) which have toppled from melting icebergs. The problem lies with sea-levels. A cold 'glacial' climate, likely to favour icebergs off Saunton, is linked to low world sea-levels (some 100 metres lower than today, see page 26). If you can think of ways of grounding an iceberg on Saunton's shore then we can think again. By the way, this is not the only foreign boulder on this coast. Twenty-one are listed on page 38. You have already walked past five of them! How many of these are located close to present sea-level?

Evidence of Glaciation

The last two million years (the Quaternary) has been a time of many dramatic changes in climate. During colder stages ice sheets expanded in many parts of the world. More locally, ice caps grew in the north and west of the British Isles and several times expanded southwards to 'invade' Southern England and threaten North Devon.

THE DEVENSIAN THREAT — 18,000 years ago

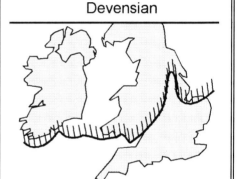
Devensian

The most recent invasion threat was towards the end of the Devensian glacial stage. At that time a 1200 metre thick ice cap spread from northern Britain as far south as the Welsh coast. North Devon, close to the edge of the ice sheet, was periglacial, experiencing a bitterly cold tundra-like climate with the average air temperature perhaps some 10°C lower than today. Freeze-thaw activity and solifluction processes caused thick foot-slope accumulations of 'head'.

THE ANGLIAN INVASION — 450,000 years ago

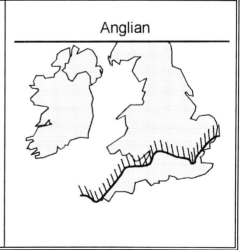
Anglian

An earlier 1800 metre thick ice sheet, the Anglian, spread further south than any other recorded. In the east it diverted the lower Thames, whilst in the west it reached the north coast of Devon and Cornwall.

It seems to have probed into Bideford Bay as far as Barnstaple. The main evidence for this is the survival of supposed glacial deposits (tills) at Fremington and Barnstaple. Here, the ice may have temporarily blocked the River Taw to create an ice-margin lake. Several far-travelled boulders (erratics) found in the glacially related deposits at Fremington are similar to those on the foreshore at Saunton, implying a common origin.

GUIDE TO LOCATING GIANT ERRATICS ON THE SAUNTON - CROYDE COAST
Paul Madgett

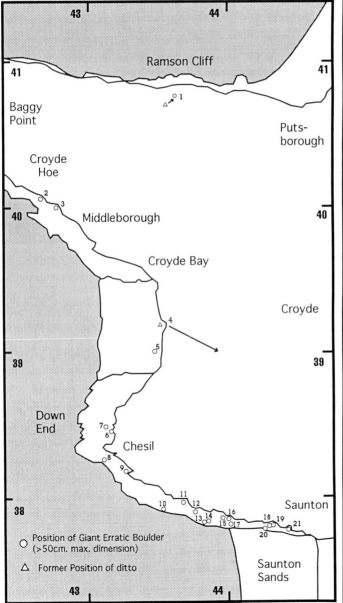

No	ROCK TYPE
1	Brown-weathered dark green EPIDIORITE
2	AGGLOMERATE
3	Black & white banded Granulite GNEISS
4	RHYOLITIC TUFF
5	GRANITE
6	Black & White banded schistose GNEISS
7	Granite GNEISS
8	Dark green META-DIORITE (?)
9	Pale green & black contorted GNEISS
10	Dark green & white DIORITE (?)
11	AMPHIBOLITE
12	QUARTZ-PORPHYRY
13	Porphyritic GRANITE
14	RHYOLITE
15	Amygdaloidal SPILITE
16	Pink/red; red veined Foliated GRANITE
17	Porphyritic MICROGRANITE
18	BRECCIATED LAVA
19	AGGLOMERATE
20	Grey/green sheared LAVA
21	Dark green/grey EPIDIORITE

O Position of Giant Erratic Boulder (>50cm. max. dimension)

△ Former Position of ditto

ax Axis	LOCATION AND COMMENT	G.R. (SS)	✓
(cm) 105	Irregularly shaped boulder at edge of clifftop path, halfway between Putsborough and NW end of Baggy Point. Originally upright at 43564070	43564075	
75	Yellow-stained boulder inside small cave. Access; cliff path W. of stream	42724005	
420	Massive boulder projects from cliff-base in 'head'. In Freshwater Gut, E. of stream. Cliff-foot access from Middleborough.	42794001	
84	Rescued from engineering works and now moved inland to Croyde.		
76	At base of beach sands. Very rarely exposed.	43553892	
135	At head of E-W gully, Down End. Access from cliff path. Until recently cemented to rocks by Raised Beach sands. (Often confused with No 7).	43183847	
120	White & black boulder in N-S gully, 50m. NNW. of No.6. Often buried	43123849	
75	Just W. of major SE-NW gully due W. of Chesil. (CARE. Access only at Low Spring Tides, over rocks S. from Down End). 49cm GRANITE nearby	43093826	
110	Near-spherical. Under large fallen block in deep gully (synclinal axis) SE of Chesil. Walk W. along base of cliffs from Saunton. CHECK TIDES.	43343813	
120	Well-rounded boulder in E-W gully close to Spring Low Water. Difficult to locate. Walk S. to low water from deep recess in cliff face.	43483793	
95	Dark green, veined boulder near cliff-base, 20m. W. of WSW-facing beach.	43683795	
150	Dark green, well-rounded. In cliff-base pool, recessed behind rock-ridge	43803793	
90	Black & white, rounded stone near seaward end of deep gully, SE from 12	43853784	
55	Rounded dark green boulder adjacent to No. 13.	43853784	
80	Rounded brown, black-speckled boulder, near head of tidal SE-trending gully. About 70m. W. of the Red Granite (No. 16).	43933787	
240	Massive rounded boulder, embedded in Raised Beach sand in cliff-base. First North Devon erratic to be described (Williams, 1837).	44013787	
125	Rounded, grey boulder, large white feldspars. Head of NW-SE tidal gully. 20m. SE of Red Granite.	44033786	
65	Dark brown/grey with rough surface. Head of NE-SW gully near cliff base.	44323782	
55	Smooth yellow/grey boulder adjacent to 18. Both No. 18 & 19 often buried.	44323782	
55	Well-rounded boulder; close to seaward end of same NE-SW gully as No.18 and No 19.	44253778	
55	Rounded with fretted surface. Near cliff-base 100m. W. of first promontory walking from Saunton.	44403780	

An old lag

Tills at Barnstaple suggest ancient glaciation. This provides a likely mechanism for transporting far-travelled boulders into the district. But if the isolated boulders at Saunton are erratics, what is their relationship to the Barnstaple till? The most obvious explanation is that the cover of till might once have been much more widespread, but that, over a long period of time, it has been largely eroded away, preserved by chance, in only one or two locations such as Fremington and Barnstaple. At Saunton, a few tough boulders remain (a lag deposit) to suggest that this site too, was once covered by glacier ice and till.

How deep was the ice here?

It would be interesting to know, but after all this time clues are scarce. However, a single large erratic (see page 39) is to be found high on Putsborough Down, 80 metres above sea-level. If ice was responsible for emplacing this isolated boulder then it points directly to an ice sheet having once overridden those cliffs and probably Saunton Down as well.

Where did the erratics come from?

The composition of most of the erratics listed match possible sources in Wales or Ireland. This fits proposed models of Anglian Stage ice movements. However, a Scottish provenance has been proposed for some erratics. This doesn't match theory as well.

Distribution pattern of erratics

Of 21 erratics listed, 20 are located on the shore platform. Is this significant? Perhaps this is the only place where they are exposed? Seaward they are not visible. Landward they may be buried beneath footslope accumulations of head deposits? However, this shoreline concentration, and the recognition of other coastal 'erratics' in South Devon and Cornwall, including a 50 tonne erratic at Porthleven, has revived interest in icebergs. The big problem is, icebergs are associated with cold stages and low sea-level (page 36). Before reading on, can you devise three natural situations where an iceberg could run aground on Saunton's shore?

Quaternary Stage	North Devon Climate	Age (years ago)
FLANDRIAN (Holocene)	Interglacial	TODAY 10,000
DEVENSIAN	Periglacial (tundra-like)	10,000 100,000
IPSWICHIAN	Interglacial	125,000
?	a cool / warm / cool complex	
HOXNIAN	Interglacial	350,000
ANGLIAN	Glacial	450,000

HOW TO FLOAT AN ICEBERG TO SAUNTON CLIFFS

1   Depress the land

Isostasy

Since the 218 metre high Hoover Dam was built across the Colorado in 1936, the weight of water ponded in the reservoir has depressed the rock floor beneath Lake Mead by 170 mm. This is an example of isostasy.

Glacio-isostasy

Similarly, during glacial stages of the Quaternary, when water loads were transferred from the oceanic 70% of the earth's surface to the glaciated 5%, the additional load of ice caused the earth's crust to be depressed (Glacio-isostasy). Ice over Greenland today is over 3000 metres thick and locally depresses the earth's crust by 1000 metres. During the most extensive glaciation of the British Isles (Anglian), the British ice cap probably exceeded a thickness of 1800 metres (1.8 km).

A depressed area

The diagram below proposes that depression of the earth's crust would have extended well beyond the edge of the ice cap. If depression was sufficient to compensate for falls in world sea-level caused by the interruption of the water cycle, then icebergs could come floating in.

One argument against this particular mechanism for erratic emplacement is that regional shoreline warping expected with glacio-isostasy seems to be absent in south-west England, as is any significant range of heights in the distribution of the shoreline erratics in Devon and Cornwall.

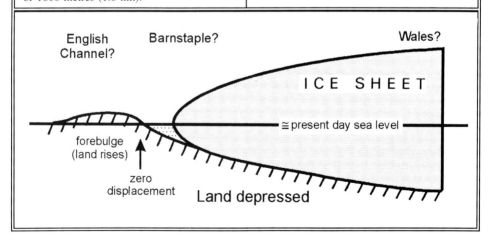

Healthy Speculation

Showing that icebergs could enter Bideford Bay is not the same thing as proving that icebergs brought the Saunton erratics. The origin of erratic coastal boulders throughout south-west England is still a matter of healthy speculation and mild controversy. Further evidence is awaited.

2   Change world sea-level

On page 26 it was suggested that, superimposed on the climatically controlled yo-yo oscillations in sea-level, might be a more long term gentle fall in world sea-level relative to the land. If this descending staircase idea (whatever the cause) is projected back in time, then it is possible to envisage circumstances in the earlier Quaternary when low 'glacial' sea-levels might match those of the present interglacial 'high'. This, it can be argued, is one way of making the iceberg theory tenable.

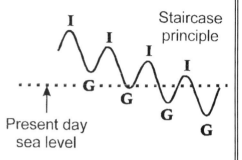

3   Have a cold snap

North Atlantic Drift
We live in northern Europe (latitude 51°N), yet we take for granted our climatically privileged position, being lapped by the warm North Atlantic Drift. If that current should fail, our climate might resemble the harshness of northern Newfoundland (51°N). Icebergs are no strangers to that coast.

Greenland Ice Project
Recent evidence from the snow of the Greenland Ice Cap, suggests that the apparently dependable, stable warmth of our present interglacial is perhaps the exception. For example, the last interglacial was marked by startling periods of instability. At one time the average temperature in Greenland dropped by 14°C within ten years. Such dramatic changes may be associated with a weakening of the North Atlantic Drift. A trail of ocean floor debris suggests that such episodes allowed the cold Greenland Current to spew erratic-laden icebergs far south into the Atlantic. If such catastrophic instability was a feature of previous interglacials, then could it be that some of the littoral erratics of south-west England arrived on or within such Trans-Atlantic visitors? The rock types found in Greenland does not rule this out.

Relevance to our lives
This is not simply at matter of academic interest. As we face a climate increasingly modified by the actions of society, an understanding of what caused instability in previous interglacials becomes of more than passing interest.

The return walk

The granite boulder marks the furthest point on this visit. On the return walk, you could consider how the cliff sites you have visited can be fitted into a logical sequence of events to tell a story of climatic and environmental change. The record sheet, on page 14, was designed to be completed during this final stage. A possible timescale for the story is provided in the table on page 40.

Try reconstructing the story yourself before turning over to the final page, which outlines the most probable scenario, according to us! Most of the dates used on the walk have been inferred from studies elsewhere but there have been attempts to date the sand-rock at Saunton, outlined below.

HOW OLD IS THE SAND-ROCK?

Amino-acid racemisation	**Thermoluminescence**
This technique is based on measuring the rate at which amino-acids in a fossil shell revert to a stable form, measured from the time of death of its inhabitant. Results hint that shells at Saunton fall into two distinct age groups. This can be interpreted in several ways: (a) two sea-level peaks during the last interglacial (Ipswichian); (b) an Ipswichian beach containing older reworked shells or (c) the presence of a second, older beach (Hoxnian?).	Grains of sand (quartz) hidden from sunlight, will accumulate radioisotopes in their matrix at a rate related to the length of time the sand has been buried. When heated in the lab, the release of radioisotopes can be measured to suggest the probable date when a deposit of sand was last buried. Preliminary results at Saunton imply that the raised beach sand dates from the last interglacial, the Ipswichian. (University of Plymouth)

Relevant debate or intellectual curiosity?

We hope that you have been stimulated by the speculation surrounding the history of the cliffs at Saunton and perhaps can apply what you have seen here to other areas to enhance your enjoyment of exploring physical landscapes. Earth scientists share a similar intellectual curiosity. They also are aware that, to modify James Hutton's statement on page 2, " The past is the key to the future". The greater our understanding of the climate of the recent geological past, the better equipped we will be to evaluate and respond to the approaching threat of dramatic climatic change.

Peter Keene and Chris Cornford.   12th October 1995.

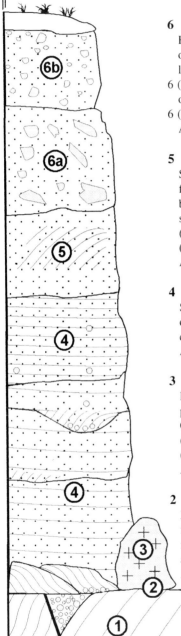

6   UPPER CLIFF

HEAD (Solifluction) slope deposits. Angular stones orientated down-slope from Saunton Down (former cliff-line). A matrix-supported unsorted deposit of local stones.

6 (b)   Upper finer head. Hill-wash of less severe climate? or, as has been claimed, a second, distinct, cold phase?

6 (a)   Lower coarser head.

AGE: Devensian Cold stage (18,000 years old)?

5   MIDDLE CLIFF

SAND-ROCK with some calcareous cementing derived from shells. Interpretation cautious but in places, dune-bedding and sand similar to modern dunes suggest fossil sand-dune complex ramped up against ancient cliff (Saunton Down). Best developed towards the western end (Down End) where raised beach apron narrowest.

AGE: Ipswichian interglacial sand-dunes (125,000 years)?

4   LOWER CLIFF

SAND-ROCK. Pebbles and shingle beds and sand deposits of former shore now a raised fossil beach with some later calcareous cementing from shelly sands.

AGE: Ipswichian interglacial beach (125,000 years)?

3   ERRATIC BOULDER

Isolated foliated granite boulder resting on raised shore platform and partly sealed in by lower cliff beach deposits. One of a series of giant erratics. Transport options?

(a)   Lag from eroded glacial till (Anglian cold stage?).

(b)   Drop-stone from grounded iceberg.

AGE: Anglian glacial cold stage (450,000 years)?

2   SHORE PLATFORM

MARINE PLATFORM cut into Pilton Shales. Raised fossil platform passes beneath later Quaternary deposits to meet now-buried former cliff line of Pilton Shales. Platform assumed to date from an earlier Quaternary interglacial.

AGE: Unknown, but older than erratics.

1   PILTON SHALES

365 million years old (Upper Devonian)
Folded & faulted shore platform.